ANCIENT ELEPHANTS

Ancient Elephants

WRITTEN AND ILLUSTRATED BY

William E. Scheele

DIRECTOR, CLEVELAND MUSEUM OF NATURAL HISTORY

CLEVELAND AND NEW YORK

THE WORLD PUBLISHING COMPANY

Published by The World Publishing Company
2231 West 110th Street, Cleveland 2, Ohio

Published simultaneously in Canada by
Nelson, Foster & Scott Ltd.

Library of Congress Catalog Card Number: 58-9421

FIRST EDITION

NO ONE who reads this book will ever
see a living mastodon or mammoth, for both
of these ancient elephants died mysteriously
and disappeared forever many thousands of
years ago.

Yet we know a great deal about these
huge animals. Prehistoric man saw living
mammoths, and many of them were killed
by ice-age hunters. Some of these hunters
were very good artists. They have left us
cave paintings and carvings which show us
how the mammoth looked.

[5]

We have also learned a lot about ancient elephants from fossil bones which have been found in all parts of the world except Australia and the farthest tip of South America. So many bones and teeth of mastodons have been found in the United States that some fossil hunters believe that these elephants were once as numerous as the buffalo of the Western plains.

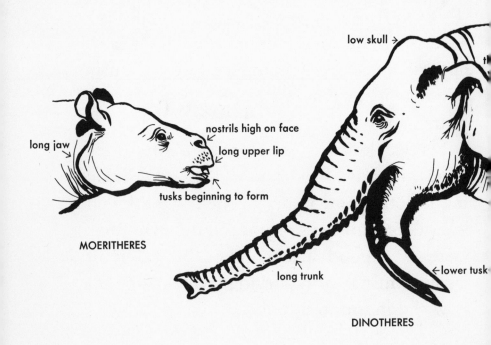

low skull →

long jaw

nostrils high on face

long upper lip

tusks beginning to form

MOERITHERES

long trunk

←lower tusk

DINOTHERES

Heads

Mastodons and mammoths became extinct about seven to fifteen thousand years ago, but they were by no means the earliest elephants. Fossil bones show clearly that elephants or their ancestors have lived on the earth for 70 million years, from the time of the last dinosaurs. There have also been many different kinds of elephants. Although only three species live in the world today,

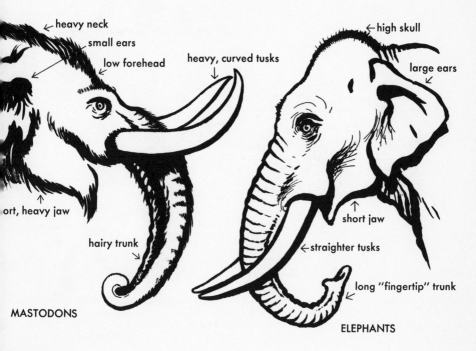

← heavy neck

small ears

low forehead

heavy, curved tusks

←high skull

large ears

ort, heavy jaw

hairy trunk

short jaw

←straighter tusks

long "fingertip" trunk

MASTODONS

ELEPHANTS

Elephant Groups

scientists are able to describe at least 600 types of elephants from fossil bones and teeth. In order to study them more easily they have divided them into eight major families.

MOERITHERIUM

MASTODON

PLATYBELODON

TRILOPHODON

Typical Ancient Elephants: O

Some ancient elephants were thin and tall; others were hairy and fat. Some had straight tusks; others had tusks like shovels or hooks. Some elephants had two tusks, some of them four. Some tusks were useless;

EUBELODON

DINOTHERIUM

LAXODONTA

STEGODON

others were used so much for digging that they were worn short or were flat and broken. But no matter how much extinct elephants varied in size or in the shapes of tusks and bones, they can usually be identified by their teeth.

The teeth of all elephants are made up of flat plates of dentine and enamel, joined by a layer of cement. The chewing surface is a series of ridges and small cones that chop any plant matter into bits. The pattern of this chewing surface is different for each kind of elephant. Scientists sort out the different species by examining the pattern of ridges or cones on the teeth.

Elephants' teeth, like those of all animals, are very hard. They are preserved as fossils more often than bones. A surprisingly large number of extinct animals are known only from their teeth.

Elephants are startling to us because of their great size. Only the largest dinosaurs

Typical Elephant Teeth

side view of molar

chewing surface

DINOTHERIUM

AMERICAN MASTODON

**TETRALOPHODON
(LONG-JAWED ELEPHANT)**

STEGODON

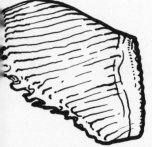 

WOOLLY MAMMOTH

and one extinct variety of rhinoceros from Asia were bigger than the ancient elephants; whales are the only mammals that are bigger than modern elephants.

These great beasts, the largest hoofed mammals alive today, eat plants. The most unusual parts of their bodies are their tusks and huge grinding teeth, the great head with its big ears and a flexible nose that we call the trunk, and their long legs that resemble pillars.

Baby elephants, modern ones and most of those that are extinct, have "baby" teeth that fall out of their jaws as the animal grows. A set of huge molars, usually one upper and one lower tooth on each side of the jaw, replace them as the animal gets older. As each tooth wears down, it is pushed forward and

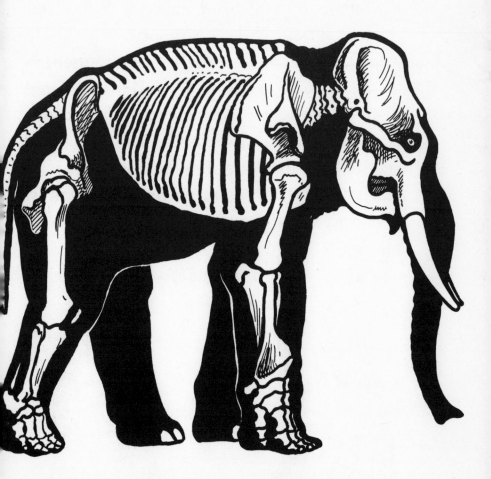

Skeleton of Indian Elephant

out of the jaw to be replaced by another. In this way, elephants grow twelve teeth in a lifetime.

Like all other animals that are tall, elephants have long bones in the upper parts of their front and hind legs. Each foot has five toes spread wide to support the animal's weight, but not all of the toes grow toenails on the outside of the foot. Under the bones of the foot there is a thick pad of cartilage that acts as a cushion for the animal's great weight. The foot of a living elephant can be nearly two feet long; larger mammoths must have had truly gigantic feet.

Foot of Indian Elephant

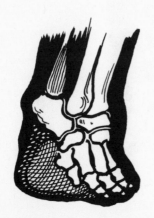 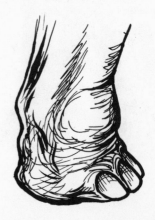

American Mastodon

Elephants are also thick-skinned. The hide is an inch or more thick and protects the animal from nearly all dangers. All elephants have some hair on their bodies, but a few, such as mastodons and woolly mammoths, had very long, thick hair all over the body. The drawings made by cave men show this, and the frozen bodies of mammoths sometimes still have hair on the hide.

In spite of the elephant's thick skin and hair, insects have always been among their worst enemies. Elephants that live in warm climates must bathe often and take mud baths to keep their thick hides from cracking and giving insect pests a chance to harm them.

Ancient elephants also searched out wet places. Many bogs contain healing minerals, and these were visited by whole herds of elephants. Some of the greatest discoveries of mastodon and mammoth bones have been made near salt licks or in soft, clay-filled bogs. The large number of fossil bones that have been dug from such spots make it clear that there were many accidents and drownings as the animals came for water, relief from insects, or to heal wounds from battles with rivals or enemies.

For many years, scientists thought India was the homeland of all elephants. Then in 1901 a fossil-hunting expedition from the British Museum found many exciting animal bones in the North African desert, not far from Cairo. Among them were parts of an animal that stood about three feet tall.

This animal, called Moeritherium (*mee·ree·thee·ree·um*) because it was found in the ancient dried-up bed of Lake Moeris, must

[16]

Moeritherium

have looked something like a small hippopotamus. It had a rather large, broad head,
and a pair of oversized teeth in each jaw.
Nostril openings were high in the skull in
the front of the face. It proved to be the
earliest elephant we know.

[17]

The high nostril openings in Moeritherium allowed the upper lip to move freely and, eventually, to lengthen. The nostrils of later elephants moved higher and higher in the face, and the long lip developed into a trunk as the animals' size increased. Since elephants are such tall animals, they need trunks for grasping and carrying leaves and twigs to their mouths. Gradually, the oversized incisor teeth became tusks in later elephants.

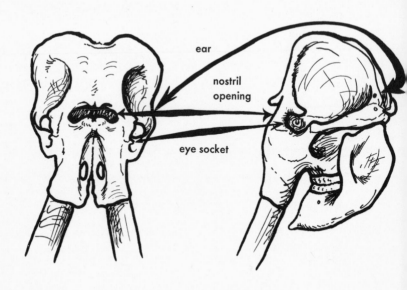

Skull of Indian Elephant

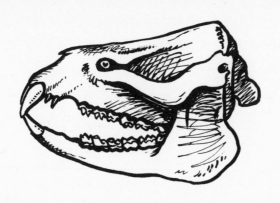

Skull of Moeritherium

Moeritherium lived successfully for about 10 million years. Several distinct sizes, ranging from one and a half feet to almost three feet in height at the shoulder, are known.

The discovery of this fossil in a dried-up lake bed indicates that it liked water and probably never left it for very long. The need and love of water is still an important part of elephant life today. It also gives us a clue to elephant relationships with other animals —hyraxes, dugongs, and manatees—that do not look or act like elephants at all.

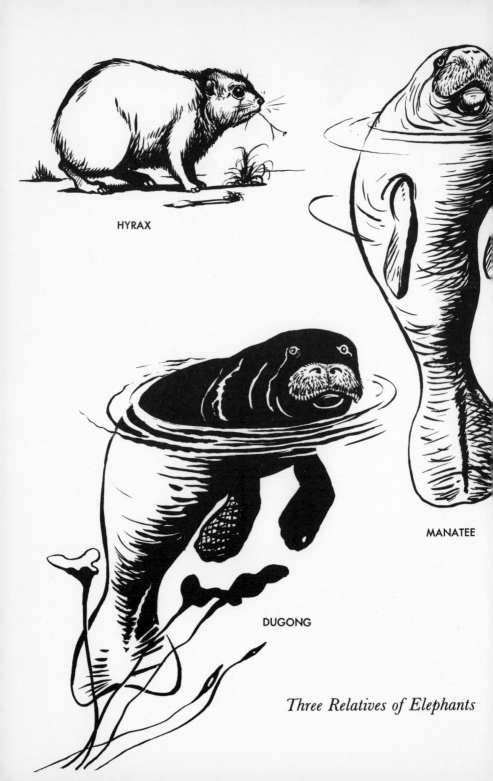

HYRAX

MANATEE

DUGONG

Three Relatives of Elephants

The bones of two other elephantlike animals were also discovered in Egypt, close to the place where the bones of the very first ancestor of all elephants were found. The bones of the animals, called Phiomia (fee·o·mee·a) and Paleomastodon (pay·lee·o·*mas*·to·don), were found among rocks that are 35 million years old.

Both animals died in a watery place, probably a broad river bed near a shallow lake. The bones of Phiomia were plentiful, which means that it was at home near water. The bones of Paleomastodon were rarer, a sign that its home was probably farther away, near the forested higher land.

Each of these animals had a short trunk which helped it grasp food, and four unusual tusks. The round, pointed tusks in the upper jaw curved forward and down.

In Phiomia, the lower tusks are long and flat. They were probably used to dig for food, and so this animal can be called the first of the "shovel-tuskers."

Phiomia

Paleomastodon is considered the ancestor of the huge mastodon of the ice-age world, but its teeth and bones are so rare that we can only guess that this is so. Unlike Phiomia, the blunt, lower tusks were short and round.

Phiomia stood about five feet five inches high at the shoulder; Paleomastodon was six feet eight inches tall. The body of each animal was probably covered with hair.

Paleomastodon

We know very little about the long-jawed elephants that lived during the next 10 million years. Almost no fossils from this period have been found, even though many elephants must have been living during that time.

Long-jawed elephants were between five and seven feet tall. Some lived in forests, some stayed near water, and others grazed on grassy plains. Many of these animals had long lower jaws, short trunks, and four tusks.

Slowly, as feeding habits changed and elephants migrated to new territories, their bodies also began to change. Longer trunks were needed by the elephants that grew taller. Species that fed upon soft-water plants

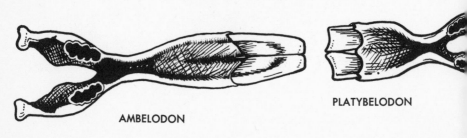

AMBELODON

PLATYBELODON

Lower Jaws of Two "Shovel-tuskers"

Trilophodon

developed spoon-shaped lower tusks. Others had short lower jaws and sharp ridged teeth that allowed them to feed on twigs in the woodlands.

There were more than a hundred different kinds of long-jawed elephants. We know from their teeth and bones which ones were most alike, but there are no direct lines of growth and evolution that can be linked together to tell us the whole story of elephants during these millions of years.

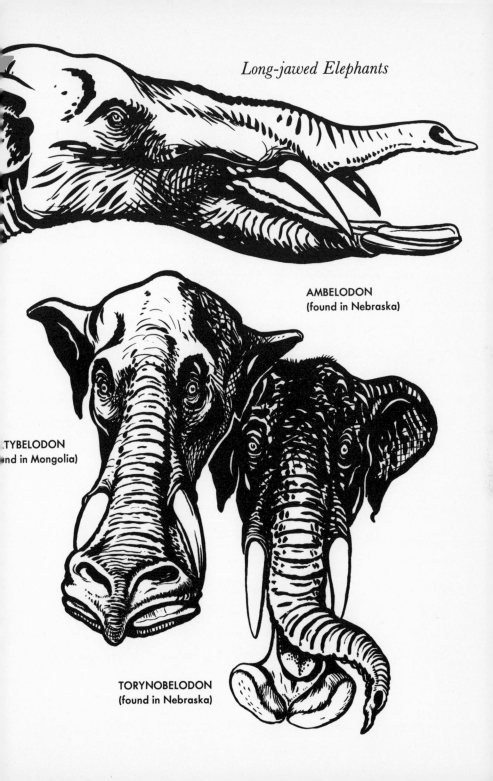

Long-jawed Elephants

AMBELODON
(found in Nebraska)

ΛTYBELODON
nd in Mongolia)

TORYNOBELODON
(found in Nebraska)

While the long-jawed elephants were spreading over most of the world, another branch of the elephant family, called Dinotheria (dy·no·*thee*·ree·a), was spreading over Asia, Europe, and North Africa. These animals lived on earth for a long time—nearly 25 million years. The only important change in their skeletons during all this time was their steady increase in size.

Dinotheria did not have upper tusks, but the tusks in the lower jaw were well developed. Instead of growing outward, they

Evolution of Dinotheres

Dinotherium

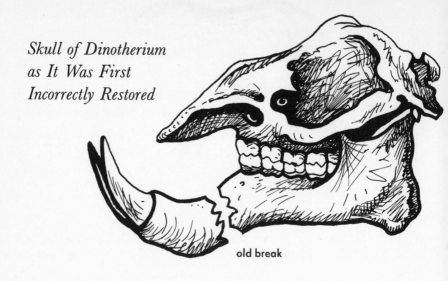

*Skull of Dinotherium
as It Was First
Incorrectly Restored*

old break

curved downward and backward like huge
hooks. The fossil tusks we have found show
no signs of wear or dullness, so their use is
not clearly understood at present. The largest of these animals lived about the same
time as mastodons and mammoths during
the late Pleistocene Epoch, or ice age. It
stood twelve feet nine inches high at the
shoulder—almost equal in size to the largest
elephants of all time. Like the mastodons
and mammoths, this animal had a long
trunk.

[30]

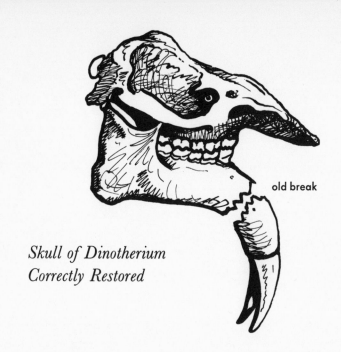

old break

Skull of Dinotherium Correctly Restored

Scientists are puzzled by the dinotheres because they are not closely related to any other elephants; they seem to have neither ancestors nor descendants. The skeleton of this animal looks very much like the skeleton of other elephants, yet its teeth are unusual, distinctly unlike those of other elephants. Bones and the skull of Dinotherium are rare. The animal has not been found in North America, and only parts of the skeleton are displayed in our museums.

Mastodons were forest-dwelling elephants that lived toward the end of the ice age about nine to twelve thousand years ago. Thousands of them have been found in many lands, but the best skeletons have been discovered in the northeastern United States which was then a cold, wet region at the edge of melting glaciers.

As the glaciers retreated to the north they left behind many lakes and bogs scattered

among hills of crushed rocks, sand, and soil.
These were soon covered by forests of evergreen trees. Wet spots in the land were
natural pits, full of sticky clay and rotting
plants. Some of the lakes were matted with
thick sphagnum moss that, as time passed,
grew out over the open water. Tamarack
trees rimmed the shores of the lakes until
they became matted tangles of dead trees
and shrubs.

American Mastodon

This forbidding wilderness was the home of the American mastodon, the largest and most common elephant of the large mastodon family. This huge barrel-shaped animal stood just under ten feet tall. It was protected from cold by thick reddish-brown hair that covered its body and grew longest on the hump of flesh over its shoulders and strong neck. Its tusks were thick, long, and sharply curved. Its forehead was more sloping than that of mammoths and modern elephants.

The mastodon was a browsing (twig-eater) animal whose teeth were ideal for cutting and chewing branches and leaves. The gummy resin of spruce trees and other evergreens is often found in the deep valleys between the numerous conical projections on the chewing surface of each mastodon tooth. Sometimes, this pitch contains pollen grains that give scientists a clue to the plants that were growing when mastodons were alive.

U. S. 1052306

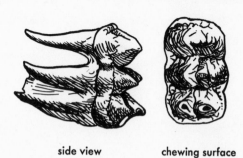

side view　　　　chewing surface

Molar of American Mastodon

GIANT BISON

SABER-TOOTHED CAT

PRONGHORN

GROUND
SLOTH

ARMADILLO

Wet and treacherous land conditions and swarms of insects probably kept the earliest human hunters away from the dark expanse of evergreen trees that covered the states near our Great Lakes. But many large animals—mammoths, lions, giant sloths and beavers, horses, camels, and huge bison—lived in these regions. Each variety had its own needs and lived near the food it ate. Mastodons probably stayed very close to the dense evergreen forests. Mammoths grazed in more open, grassy flatland.

Swamps and bogs were ideal food producers for mastodons, but they were death traps too. Animals that were driven to seek relief and protection from insects by mudbathing were often caught in these soft-bottomed, natural pits. The sticky blue-gray clay held them upright as the pond rubbish filled around the upper body and head. The brown water of most bogs is full of acids that help preserve bones; this is one reason for the many perfectly preserved skeletons of mastodons in our museums.

Mastodon bones were found in America as early as 1705, and Thomas Jefferson himself collected them from the famous "elephant graveyard" at Big Bone Lick in Kentucky. Since then thousands of mastodons have been uncovered in this country.

The three most famous skeletons are remarkable because they are so complete. They are the Warren Mastodon in the American Museum of Natural History in New York City, the Whitfield skeleton sold to the Frankfort Museum in Germany, and the Johnstown Mastodon in the Cleveland Museum of Natural History. All three skeletons came from bogs in which the living

Dredging an Ice-age Bog

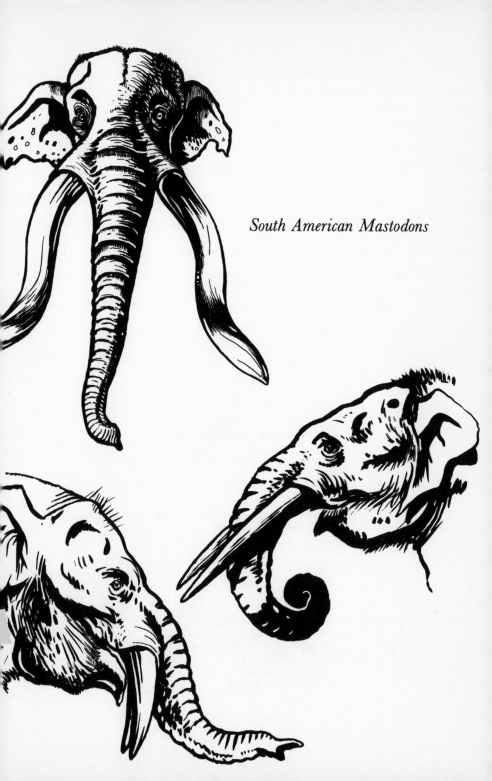

South American Mastodons

animal had drowned and was held fast in an upright position by clay.

The Johnstown fossil was discovered in Ohio by a young farm hand who was looking for an easy place to bury two dead pigs. He chose the wet black soil of a pasture and had just begun to dig when his shovel struck an object that proved to be an elephant's tusk. Excitedly, he dug further and soon realized that he had made an important discovery.

Almost all the bones of this mastodon were recovered; only a few tail bones and the breastbone were missing. Unfortunately, souvenir hunters took some of the toe bones before they could be protected properly.

When the mastodon was mounted on an iron framework, it became clear that it had been seriously injured some time before it died. The last six ribs on the left side had been broken and healed, the pelvis was badly nicked, and eight of the vertebrae in its back were twisted and swollen. This wound was probably made by the tusk of another elephant. The Johnstown bones were those of a young bull about nineteen years old; it is possible that an older male defeated him in a fight and drove him from the herd.

Specialists who examined the lump of bone that grew along the mastodon's injured back think that this animal suffered from arthritis. All other body parts were in

[41]

a healthy condition, but the injury to ribs and backbone must have caused the elephant to limp for the rest of his life. A long time after the gaping back wound had healed, the unfortunate beast entered a bog to rest and feed. Its weight was too great for the ice or vegetation that covered the bog water, and the mastodon drowned. He was not strong enough to escape his death.

Mastodon bones are the most common elephant fossils, but the remains of mammoths are more widely scattered throughout the world. They are found in a greater number of countries, and there were more different kinds of them.

Ancient elephants made some of the greatest migrations known to the animal world, but mammoths were the greatest travelers of all. They migrated in herds to and from feeding grounds that were hundreds of miles apart.

The first mammoths came from South Africa. Gradually, they migrated north into Europe and then east through Asia to the land bridge that connected North America and Asia late in the ice age.

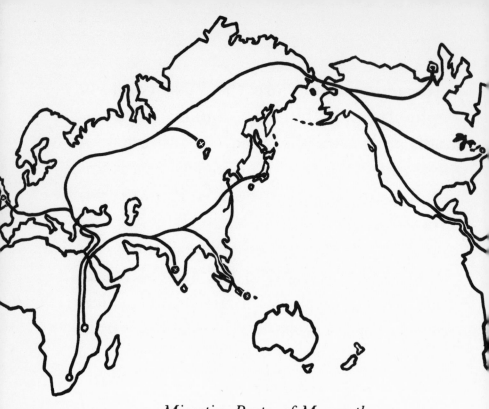

Migration Routes of Mammoths

From Alaska, the mammoths came south into the central United States, where the grassy plains fed them well. The tallest mammoths found in this country lived in what is now the State of Nebraska. They then spread southward into Mexico and Central America and as far as northern South America where the trail ends, 15,000 miles from its starting point.

It took 3 million years for mammoths to spread from Africa to South America. Along the way, the slow changes of time and breeding produced different types and a steady increase in size. Their fossil bones and the art of ice-age man show us that mammoths were one of the most spectacular animals our world has ever known.

*Ivory
Mammoth*

Prehistoric hunters knew mammoths well, for they have left us many carvings and paintings that give a clear picture of the animals. The most famous paintings are drawn on cave walls in France and Spain. In Africa, hunters carved their animal pictures on steep rock walls and then rubbed color into the grooves and scratches to make them show clearly.

Mammoths in Ice-age Art

Ice-age men hunted and successfully killed mammoths. Scientists have discovered large killing-stones, elephant pits, and spear points in Europe and America that were used for this purpose, and many ice-age tools were made from elephant ivory and bones.

Killing a mammoth with spears was a difficult job, but primitive hunters soon learned to take advantage of elephant migrations. They camped at well-known passes, waiting for the mammoths to come through valleys where they could kill them more easily.

Spear Points Used To Kill Mammoths

One of the most famous of these camps
was discovered in Czechoslovakia at an important passage place between the Danube
River valley and the Northern European
plains. Great herds of game passed this point
twice a year during the spring and fall migration seasons. Primitive hunters lived there

year after year, killing enough woolly mammoths at each migration to fill their needs. The bones of at least a thousand mammoths were found at this camp site.

Other mammoth hunter camps have been discovered in Austria, Russia, and the United States.

Woolly Mammoth

The woolly mammoth was not the largest mammoth, but it is probably the best known. This vigorous animal stood just over nine feet high and had a long trunk and small ears. It lived in the far north among polar bears, musk oxen, and wolves and was able to survive the bitter cold because of its thick skin, a deep layer of body fat, and its hairy body. Specimens of this mammoth that have been found in the frozen earth of arctic regions show that its hair was a light yellowish-brown wool with long black hair growing through the undercoat. On certain parts of the body, this hair was about two feet long.

The body fat was a reserve supply of food that was used up by the animal during the hard northern winters. One of these lumps of fat collected on the high round forehead of the woolly mammoth. Drawings made by cave men show this animal looking lean and small-headed in summer, high-headed in winter; the difference is due to the thickness of fat on the forehead.

Mammoths that lived in the north ate the grasses and dwarf plants that still grow on the tundra today. Poppies, ferns, and arctic willows have been found in the stomachs of

winter   summer

Woolly Mammoth

several frozen specimens. One remarkable specimen still had twenty-four pounds of food between its teeth when it was discovered. This mammoth died so suddenly that it had no time to swallow its food.

Most elephants use their tusks for digging food, but mammoths did not. Their long, slender tusks grew in a sweeping circle that often overlapped at the tusk points.

The largest tusk on record is sixteen feet five inches long; many others average between eleven and thirteen feet in length. These huge tusks were set in a skull that was longer than the skull of a mastodon or most other elephants. The hips and hind legs of mammoths were not as strong as those of other elephants because they did not use them for pushing the tusks into the earth, digging for food.

TUSKS OF
AFRICAN ELEPHANT

TUSKS OF
WOOLLY MAMMOTH

Mossbach Giant Mammoth

Mammoths of the warmer lands were the
tallest elephants known. They were much
larger than the northern species. Their legs
were long, and their bodies were thinner.
Their thin tusks were longer, too, and their
ears were larger. Like all mammoths, their
teeth were flat grinders, ideal for smashing
tough grasses.

[54]

Like the mastodons, mammoths disappeared from the earth as the ice age ended. The changes in weather that caused the glaciers to melt also affected plant life. It is possible that woolly mammoths, the plant eaters of the north, starved to death because they needed more food than they could find. We know that they died out rather quickly. Perhaps the starving parents could not protect the weak young animals from wolves and other enemies. Mammoths living in warmer climates apparently did not die out until much later.

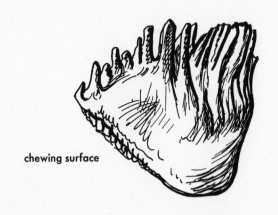

chewing surface

Upper Molar of Mammoth

Imperial
Mammoth

Skeletons of woolly mammoths are so numerous that in Siberia parts of several hundred frozen animals have been found every year for centuries. For hundreds of years, the Russians have collected the bones, teeth, and tusks of mammoths and sold them for use as carving ivory. Mammoth ivory is still one of their important export products.

The remains of woolly mammoths are commonly found in boggy or frozen ground. Nearly all other kinds of mammoth bones are found in the water-washed sands and soil of rivers which the tall elephants followed during their migrations.

Skull of Woolly Mammoth

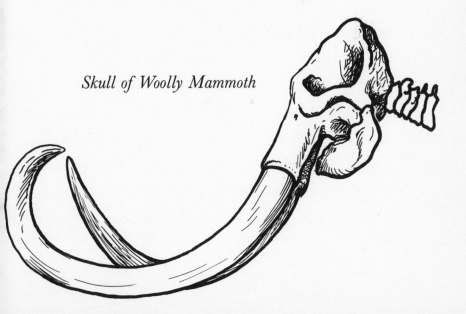

Full skeletons of these mammoths are seldom found, for river water was usually deep and powerful, and the skeletons were torn apart and scattered by the currents. Very often, only the heavy tusks and lower parts of the skull are still fixed in place when a specimen is discovered. The upper part of the mammoth's skull was full of air pockets in the bone, which enlarged the head and provided a flat surface to which the neck muscles were attached. Because it was so large, the skull often stuck out of the ground like a boulder as the body of the dead mam-

[58]

moth was being covered by earth. Often, this portion was crushed and lost. The top of the skull in nearly all museum mammoths, therefore, is made of plaster of Paris.

The fragile tusks fared better, however, because the dry sandy soil of old river beds, which allows wetness to drain away, helped preserve them. Tusks found in wet, clayey places often fall apart when exposed to air and sunlight.

Stegodon

Two Asiatic Ancestors of the Indian Elephant

Of the hundreds of kinds of elephants that once lived, only three kinds are living today. These are the Asiatic elephant, the African elephant, and a pygmy African elephant. The teeth, tusks, ears, head shape, and body size of each of these animals are quite different. The African elephants eat twigs and coarse plants. The Asiatic, or Indian, elephant prefers to eat grasses.

AFRICAN ELEPHANT   INDIAN ELEPHANT

INDIAN

AFRICAN

These beasts are impressive to see and curious to study, but they are relics of the ice age that are doomed to disappear unless they are protected.

This will not be an easy job. Wild elephants need a wide range to live on, and they are destructive to the crops of farmers. Elephants also reproduce slowly. If they are confined to game preserves and zoos, there will have to be a great number of breeding captives to keep them from dying out.

Like the giraffe, the rhinoceros, the hippopotamus, and many kinds of antelopes that are now all isolated in Africa, living elephants mark the end of a long parade of great beasts whose ancestors roamed the

[62]

prehistoric world. They give us a fascinating glimpse into the ancient past when our own ancestors were still living in caves and mastodons and mammoths were the monarchs of the ice age.

Indian Elephant

WILLIAM E. SCHEELE, Director of the Cleveland Museum of Natural History, was born in Cleveland in 1920. He won scholarships in art and biology and was graduated from Western Reserve University in 1947. In November, 1939, he won the first annual Bird Art Contest, sponsored by the Cleveland Museum of Natural History, and the next day he was a member of their staff. In 1949, after army service had interrupted his career, he was appointed director of the museum; he is one of the youngest museum directors in the country. Mr. Scheele's outside activities include painting natural-history subjects (he has exhibited in many museums), gem cutting, and fossil hunting. He lives with his wife and three sons on a tree farm near Chardon, Ohio.

1 2 3 4 5 6 7 8 9 10 67 66 65 64 63 62 61 60 59